POLAR BEAR, WHY IS YOUR WORLD MELTING?

Robert E. Wells

ARCTIC
TEMPERATURE
ALERT

Albert Whitman & Company, Morton Grove, Illinois

For my stepson, Kevin, and daughter-in-law, Bobbi, dedicated practitioners of the art of living green.

Library of Congress Cataloging-in-Publication Data

Wells, Robert E.
Polar bear, why is your world melting? / Robert E. Wells.
p. cm.
ISBN 978-0-8075-6598-8 (hardback) — ISBN 978-0-8075-6599-5 (pbk.)
1. Greenhouse effect, Atmospheric—Juvenile literature. 2. Global warming—Juvenile literature.
3. Ice—Arctic regions—Juvenile literature. I. Title.
QC912.3.W45 2008 363.738'74—dc22 2008001308

The title is hand-lettered by Robert E. Wells.
The illustration media are pen and acrylic.
Design by Carol Gildar.

For more information about Albert Whitman & Company,
please visit our web site at www.albertwhitman.com.

Also by Robert E. Wells:

Can You Count to a Googol?

Did a Dinosaur Drink This Water?

How Do You Know What Time It Is?

How Do You Lift a Lion?

Is a Blue Whale the Biggest Thing There Is?

What's Faster Than a Speeding Cheetah?

What's Older Than a Giant Tortoise?

What's Smaller Than a Pygmy Shrew?

The Arctic Ocean is very cold—
so cold it's covered with floating sea ice.
But it's just right for polar bears.

Polar bears live on the ice and hunt for seals.

Like other places in the world, the Arctic has seasons.
The winters there are long and cold. The summers are
shorter and warmer—but you still need winter clothes!

In the summer, some SEA ICE melts and breaks up
into smaller chunks called ice floes.

Now scientists are worried. Every year, the Arctic temperature has been slowly rising, and more and more summer ice has been melting.

The ice floes are getting smaller and farther apart.

ARCTIC
TEMPERATURE
ALERT

It is harder for the polar bears to hunt, and they often go hungry.

Weakened by hunger, some bears—especially mothers with cubs—are having trouble swimming the longer distances between ice floes.

We want to rescue them!

Why are the polar bears in trouble?
Why is the ice melting?
Why is the Arctic getting warmer?

The answer begins with the sun.

OUR SUN

is the energy source for all the world's weather.

It beams its hot rays all the way to Earth, 93 million miles away.

Some of the heat is reflected back into space by Earth's surface.

Some of the heat is trapped and stored by invisible GASES in the ATMOSPHERE.

The heat-trapping gases are called GREENHOUSE GASES.

They keep the air close to Earth warm.

This warming is called

THE GREENHOUSE EFFECT.

Earth's greenhouse effect warms the air like a garden greenhouse. When the sun shines through the glass or plastic of the greenhouse,

heat is trapped inside by the roof and walls.

If just the right amount of heat stays inside, plants will grow—

even when it's cold outside.

When the sun shines through the Earth's atmosphere, heat is trapped by greenhouse gases.

The main greenhouse gases that store heat are CARBON DIOXIDE, or CO_2; METHANE; NITROUS OXIDE; and WATER VAPOR.

With the right amount of these gases, Earth's AVERAGE TEMPERATURE stays at about 59 degrees Fahrenheit, or 15 degrees Celsius— just right for plants, animals, and people.

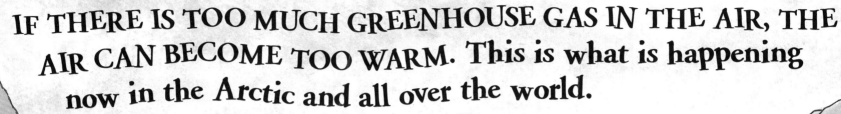

IF THERE IS TOO MUCH GREENHOUSE GAS IN THE AIR, THE AIR CAN BECOME TOO WARM. This is what is happening now in the Arctic and all over the world.

PURPLE HILLS
COAL
MINE

Scientists believe that CO_2, which stays in the air longer than the other greenhouse gases, is the main cause of the extra warming.

Much of that CO_2 comes from factories and machines that burn FOSSIL FUELS.

COAL and OIL are fossil fuels. They come from plants and tiny animals that lived long ago and became buried in the ground.

Chunks of coal from mines are loaded into train cars . . .

and transported to coal-burning factories and power plants. Coal-burning power plants generate much of the world's electricity.

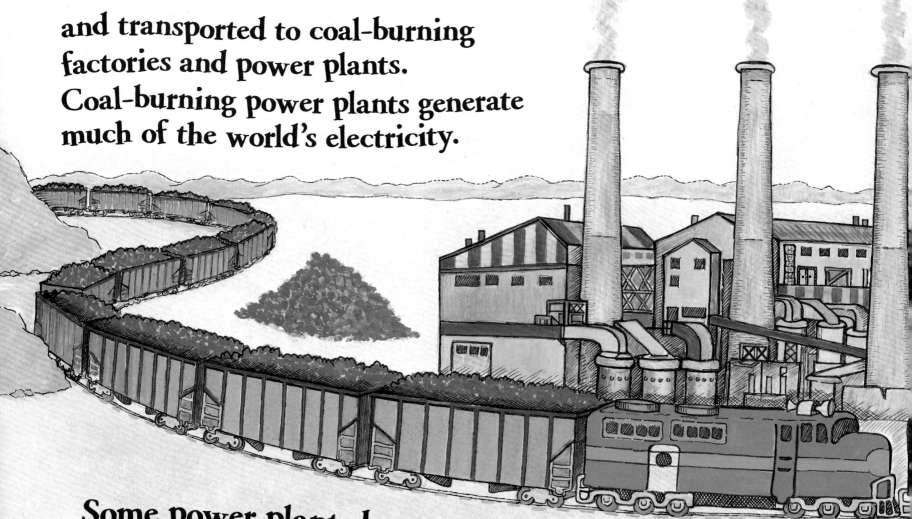

Some power plants burn more than 100 railroad carfuls of coal every day!

The world is using more and more electricity for homes, offices, and factories.

As more coal is burned to generate more electricity, more CO_2 goes into the air.

CO₂ also comes from burning oil.

Oil is pumped up from deep under the ground . . .

OIL →

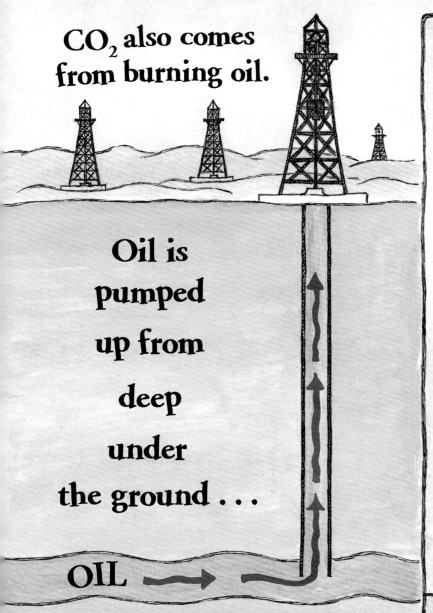

and refined into diesel fuel and gasoline for motor vehicles, boats, and ships; and kerosene for jet airplanes.

Every day, thousands of airplanes fly to cities around the world,

and thousands of ships sail across oceans and lakes.

Every day, millions of cars, trucks, buses, and motorcycles travel the world's roads and highways.

There are about 700 million cars in the world.

If they were stacked on platforms, 3 cars to a platform,

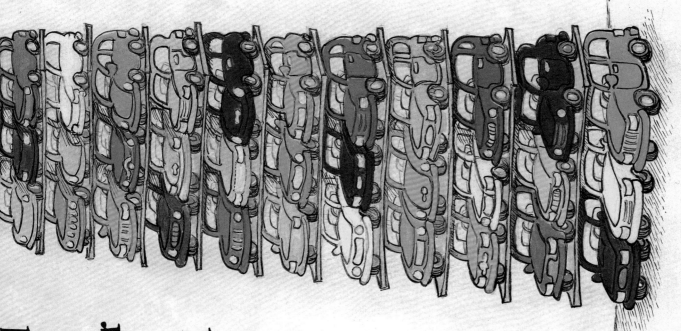

they would make a tower that reached from Earth to the moon!

The exhaust from all the world's cars goes into the air, increases the greenhouse effect, and causes more polar ice to melt!

Is it really so important to people that the Arctic ice is melting? Yes, BECAUSE ARCTIC ICE HELPS REGULATE WEATHER ALL OVER THE WORLD!

Because ice is white, it reflects the sun's heat back into space, keeping the whole world cooler.

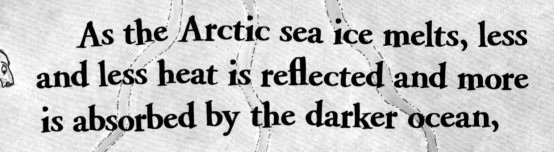

As the Arctic sea ice melts, less and less heat is reflected and more is absorbed by the darker ocean,

making the ocean warmer.

Arctic Ocean

Atlantic Ocean

As the Arctic Ocean warms, it circulates heat to other oceans,

and the water warms the air above it.

The extra heat in the air can cause weather changes—and many problems.

If forest HABITATS get too warm, trees can weaken, making it easier for insects and disease to destroy them.

If water habitats get too warm for fish, they can become ill and die.

Changing weather patterns can cause floods and EROSION in places that are usually dry,

and drought, or dryness, in places that are usually wet.

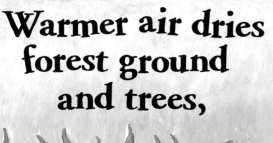

Warmer air dries forest ground and trees,

making it easier for fires to start.

The melting of glaciers and other land ice

raises ocean levels, which will also cause flooding.

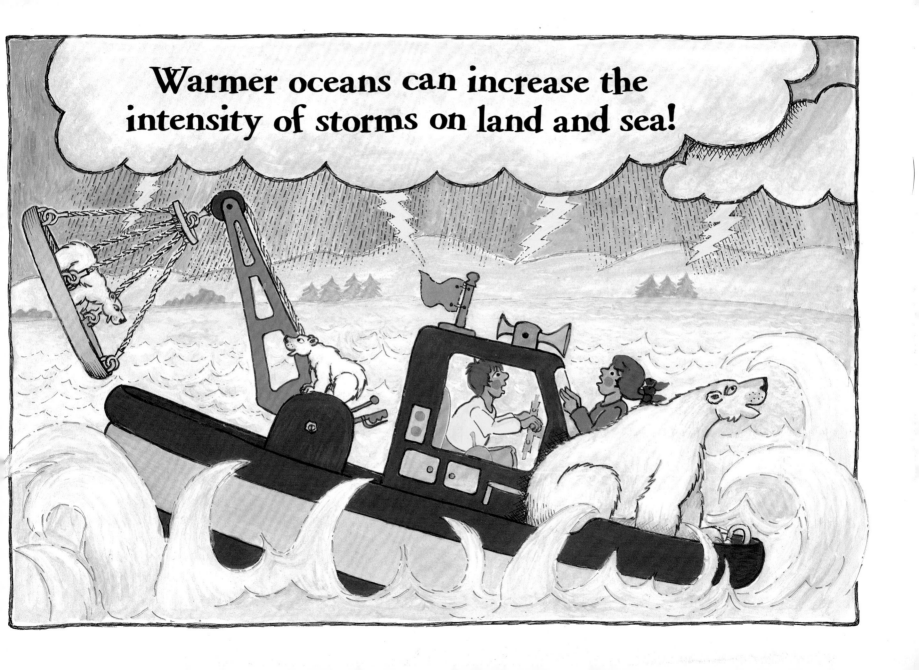

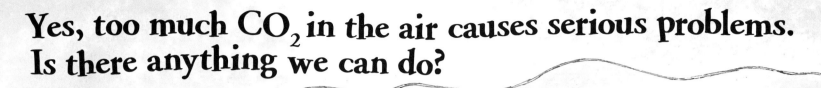

Yes, too much CO_2 in the air causes serious problems. Is there anything we can do?

Plants and trees absorb CO_2 from the air as they grow. So planting new trees can be one way to help.

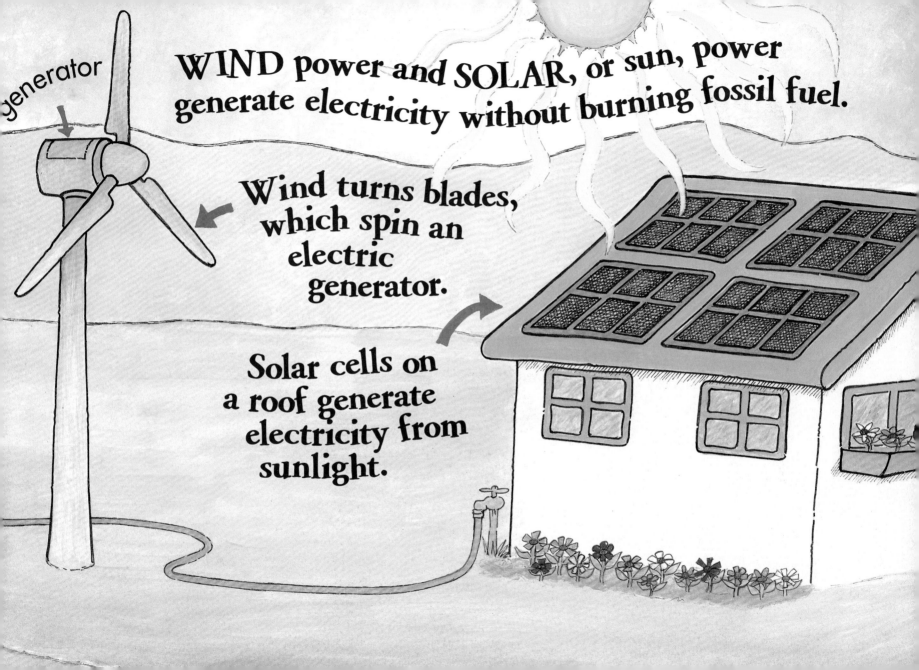

generator

WIND power and SOLAR, or sun, power generate electricity without burning fossil fuel.

Wind turns blades, which spin an electric generator.

Solar cells on a roof generate electricity from sunlight.

These are some good electricity-saving ideas:

Put a sweater on

instead of turning up the heat.

Dry clothes with the sun.

Recycle.

Even if your electricity comes from the power of the wind or the sun, conserving all electricity usually reduces CO_2 because unused electricity can be sold to other places.

Buy energy-efficient appliances.

Use energy-saving lights.

A well-insulated house needs less heat in the winter and less air-conditioning in the summer.

We can reduce CO_2 in the air by the way we travel.

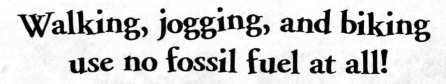

Carpooling uses less fuel per person than driving alone.

Walking, jogging, and biking use no fossil fuel at all!

With less CO_2 in the air, our world will be a cooler, healthier place for people . . .

and polar bears!

Earth's Warm Blanket

Earth's ATMOSPHERE surrounds us like a blanket. It's made up of GASES, invisible substances that have no shape or volume, and tend to expand without limits. Our atmosphere is mostly made up of the gases nitrogen and oxygen, with smaller amounts of the GREENHOUSE GASES mixed in.

The greenhouse gas WATER VAPOR does not stay in the air long—it comes back to Earth as rain and snow. NITROUS OXIDE, another greenhouse gas, occurs in the atmosphere naturally, but the amount has greatly increased over the years by the use of fertilizers on farms, the burning of forests to clear land, and the burning of fossil fuels. METHANE comes from decaying organic matter. It traps more heat in the air than CO_2, but is less of a problem for global warming, because there is much less of it—and, like water vapor, it does not stay in the air as long as CO_2, which can stay in the air for 100 years!

Ice and snow act in different ways to affect Earth. When LAND ICE, such as glaciers, melts or slides into the ocean, ocean levels rise, which can cause flooding and EROSION, the wearing away of land. When SEA ICE melts, it does not raise ocean levels, because sea ice is already floating in the ocean, but it affects temperatures.

To find EARTH'S AVERAGE TEMPERATURE, measurements are taken from different places all over the world. It is the rising of this average temperature that concerns climate scientists. Rising temperatures affect HABITATS, areas or environments where plants or animals naturally live and grow. Earth's habitats are all connected and very delicately balanced.

Our planet is sometimes called a "Goldilocks" world—not too hot, not too cold, but just right for plants, animals, and people. We must all work together to keep it this way—just right for all living things!